GIRLS' GUIDES

Body Talk

A Girl's Guide to What's Happening to Your Body

● **Victoria F. Shaw** ●

the rosen publishing group's
rosen central
new york

To Camille

Published in 1999 by The Rosen Publishing Group, Inc.
29 East 21st Street, New York, NY 10010

First Edition

Library of Congress Cataloging-in-Publication Data

Shaw, Victoria.
    Body talk: : a girl's guide to what's happening to your body / by
Victoria Shaw.
      p.   cm.
    Includes bibliographical references and index.
    Summary: Provides an overview of the physical and emotional
changes brought about by puberty in girls.
    ISBN 0-8239-2977-9
    1. Teenage girls—Physiology—Juvenile literature. 2. Puberty—literature.
[1. Puberty.   2. Teenage girls. 3. Sex
instruction for girls.] I. Title.
RJ144.   S53 1999
612.6'61'08352—dc21   89-37641
                                               CIP

Manufactured in the United States of America

Contents

About This Book

The middle school years are like a roller coaster—wild and scary but also fun and way cool. One minute you're way, way up there, and the next minute you're plunging down into the depths. Not surprisingly, sometimes you may find yourself feeling confused and lost. Not to worry, though. Just like on the roller coaster ride, at the end of all this crazy middle school stuff, you'll be laughing and screaming and talking about how awesome it all was.

Right now chances are that your body is changing so much that it's barely recognizable, your old friends may not share your interests anymore, your life at school is suddenly hugely complicated. And let's not even get into the whole boy issue. It's a wonder that you can still think straight at all.

Fortunately, reader dear, help is here. This book is your road map. It's also a treasure chest filled with ideas and advice. Armed with this book and with your own inner strength (trust us, you have plenty), you can safely, confidently navigate the twists and turns of your middle school years. It will be tough going, and sometimes you'll wonder if you'll ever get through it. But you—fabulous, powerful, unique you—are up to the task. This book is just a place to start.

Dear Vicky,

Help! I think I've caught an exotic disease. My whole body is changing. I'm growing taller by the second, and my feet are HUGE. My nipples are dark and swollen, and there's hair growing between my legs. Do you think it's fatal?

-Freaked Out!

Dear Freaked,

Chill out! You're not dying; you're going through puberty. Your body is changing from a girl's body to a woman's body. Puberty happens to all girls sooner or later. The best thing to do is sit back and enjoy the ride.

In the preteen and teen years, girls go through some pretty serious physical and emotional changes. These changes are known as puberty. During puberty a girl's body develops from a child's to a woman's body. In just a few years, you'll grow to your full adult height and foot size. You'll develop breasts and pubic hair. You'll get your period.

Luckily puberty usually happens a little at a time, so

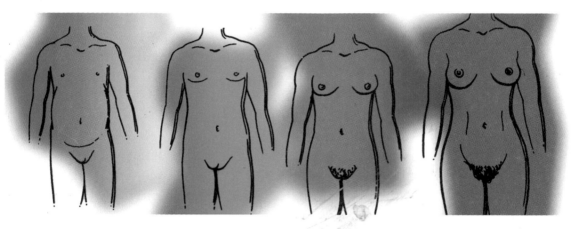

you'll have a chance to get used to the new you. And unlike our friend "Freaked," you probably won't be completely surprised by these changes. Chances are you already know at least a little bit about what happens during puberty. Of course, that doesn't mean that you don't still have lots of questions.

For most girls puberty starts between their eleventh and twelfth birthdays. But some girls begin to develop when they're only nine or ten years old. Others don't start until they're fourteen or even older. If you haven't noticed any changes yet, don't worry. You will. Everyone goes through puberty at her own special time and in her own special way.

Everyone feels differently about puberty. Some girls are totally psyched when their breasts start developing or when they get their period. Other girls feel embarrassed and uncomfortable with these changes. Girls who develop early are often teased by other kids. And puberty can be pretty scary if you're not sure what's going on. All of these feelings are completely normal. Most girls experi- ence a wide range of feel- ings at this time.

During puberty many girls start to feel differently about them- selves and the people around them. You may find that you're more concerned with what your friends are thinking and doing. You may worry more about the way you look. You might have your first crush. For some girls these feelings can be pretty intense.

This book deals with *everything ya ever wanted ta know* about puberty and your body: how to buy a bra that fits, how to tell the difference between antiperspirant and deodorant, how to deal with getting your period, and more. With luck, the book will answer all of your burning questions. But just in case it doesn't, at the end you'll find an info-packed list of books, Web sites, and other resources for learning more about your changing body.

QUIZ:

ARE YOU GOING THROUGH PUBERTY?

Have you noticed any of the following changes in your body?

✔ My feet are growing really fast.

✔ If I keep growing taller, at this rate I'll be a shoo-in for the WNBA.

✔ My breasts are starting to grow, and/or the skin around my nipples is turning a darker color.

✔ My hair and skin are more oily than they used to be.

✓ The hair on my arms and legs is growing thicker and darker in color.

✓ I feel as if I've bought a one-way ticket to Zitsville.

ADMIT ONE ZITSVILLE

✓ There is hair growing in my armpits, and my body odor smells kind of funky.

✓ There are curly pubic hairs growing between my legs.

✓ I've noticed some wetness (aka vaginal discharge) in my undies.

✓ I've started my period.

ANSWERS:

If you said "yes" to any of these questions, chances are you are starting to go through puberty. If you haven't noticed any of these changes yet, don't worry: You have plenty of time. Everyone goes through puberty at her own pace. For instance, some girls go from flat-as-a-board to a B or C cup seemingly overnight, while others develop a lot more slowly. That's the way puberty works.

Your Changin' Bod

For some girls the first sign of puberty is that they start growing pubic hairs on the vulva (translation: the outside parts of your vagina). For others it's when their breasts begin to develop. The real work of puberty happens inside of you, when your reproductive organs, or sex organs (translation: the ones involved in making babies), start producing hormones that set the rest of the process in motion.

Ages and Stages

There are actually five stages of puberty, which overlap with each other. Although girls pass through the stages at different ages, the order is the same for everyone. We'll talk more about what happens during these stages throughout the book. But here's a quick preview:

Stage #1

occurs between the ages of eight and eleven. It takes place inside of you, so you won't even know that it's happening. Your ovaries (translation: organs that hold ova, or eggs) will grow and start producing hormones.

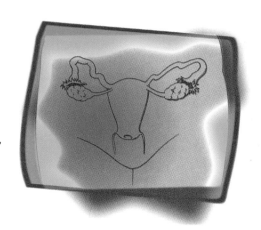

Stage #2

usually begins between the ages of eight and fourteen. (Eleven to twelve years old is average.) A lot happens during this stage. You will probably notice the initial signs of pubic hair development. These first hairs are typically very fine and straight. Your nipples will start to stick out, and they may be sensitive when touched. You may also notice that your areolas (translation: the circles of darker skin around your nipples) grow bigger. During stage 2, most girls experience a growth spurt in height and weight.

Stage #3

generally happens between the ages of nine and fifteen. (The average age is twelve to thirteen.) Your breasts will continue to develop, and your pubic hair will get coarser and darker. Your hips, pelvis, and vagina will widen, and you may get your period.

Stage #4

takes place in most girls between their tenth and sixteenth birthdays. (The average age is thirteen to fourteen.) Your pubic hair will start to form a triangle over and around your vulva, and your breasts will continue to grow. You will probably also notice that there is hair growing in your armpits. If you didn't get your period in stage 3, you will now. Inside, your ovaries are enlarging, and you may start ovulating. (See chapter four.)

Stage #5

is the grand finale of puberty, usually occurring between ages twelve and nineteen. Your periods will become regular, and you will reach your full height and breast size. Physically, at least, you'll be an adult (even though you may not feel like one).

Grow, Girl!

If the pants you bought last month are starting to look like capris or your brand-new shoes are already kinda snug, chances are you're beginning to go through puberty. For most girls puberty begins with a growth spurt during which they grow bigger and taller at a superfast pace.

Growth Spurt

The average girl starts growing like a root sometime between her eleventh and twelfth birthdays. This growth spurt usually lasts about a year, and most girls reach their full adult height one to three years after they get their period. If you're taller than all the guys in your class, you've probably already figured out that boys' growth spurts generally happen later.

As you grow taller, you may notice

something else: The shape of your body will also be changing. During puberty your pelvic bones will get bigger and broader, and fat will form on your hips and thighs. In other words, you'll develop a more womanly figure, with curves instead of straight lines.

FYI: Gaining weight during this time is totally normal. In fact, the average girl gains from forty to fifty pounds between ages ten and fourteen. Some girls gain as much as twenty pounds in a year or less.

As you gain weight, you will also be getting taller. But your height and weight don't always increase at the same pace. There may be times when you gain pounds faster than inches (or the other way around). Don't stress about this. Things will most likely even out soon.

Am I Fat?

Some girls freak and worry that they are getting fat when their figure starts to change. But you're supposed to put on weight during puberty. Girls' bodies need some fat to jump-start puberty and menstruation. And don't even think about dieting! Dieting during puberty can stunt your growth, wreck your bones, and mess with your mind.

Mature women naturally have more fat

on their bodies than men. Extra fat is your body's way of making sure that someday you will be able to carry and feed a baby.

Of course, this doesn't mean that you should go food-crazy. Try to eat a balanced diet of nutrition-packed foods like fruits, vegetables, low-fat dairy products, and lean meats. Go easy on the junk foods: soda, cookies, ice cream, chips, burgers, and fries, etc. These have tons of calories and not much in the way of nutrition. And don't be a couch potato! Go for a brisk walk with a pal or try a new sport. Exercise is a great way to keep your changin' bod in tip-top shape.

Your Feelings

Some girls are psyched when their figure starts changing, but many are not. The sad truth is that too many girls think that having hips and breasts is unattractive. Part of the problem is that the media—advertisements, movies, and TV shows—tend to glamorize superthin women. You know, the ones who have the bodies of eight-year-olds (which is fine if you're eight. . .). But after puberty most women aren't supposed to look like little girls. Don't let yourself be brainwashed by these unrealistic media images.

Your Breasts: An Owner's Manual

Breasts come in many different shapes and sizes. You may worry that yours are too big, too small, too pointy, or too droopy. But there is no one way that your breasts are supposed to be. Everyone is unique, and that goes for breasts too.

Check out the figures below to see which of the five stages of breast development you're in now. As you can see, breasts start out as bumps (aka breast buds) behind the nipples. Then the areolas and breasts continue to grow until they reach their adult size and shape. For many girls the nipple and areola start to stick out from the rest of the breast. As they develop, you may notice that your breasts look more pointy than rounded or that one breast is growing way ahead of the other. Relax! These are normal stages in breast development.

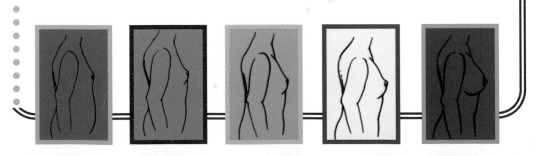

Is It Bra Time?

Do you need a bra? There's no right answer to this question. Some girls are aching to start wearing a bra. Maybe their breasts are starting to develop or maybe not, but they're definitely ready to lose those babyish undershirts. Other girls just aren't into bras. Even after their breasts have developed, they prefer to go bra-less. For girls with large breasts, this is not the best idea; the tissue that supports the breasts can tear, causing them to sag. But either way, wearing or not wearing a bra should be your decision.

If you've decided that it's bra time for you, here's what you need to know: Bra sizes have numbers and letters. The number (30, 32, 34, 36, 38, 40, etc.) is the measurement in inches around the rib cage. The letter (AA, B, C, DD, etc.) refers to the cup size (the size of your breasts). AAA is the smallest, and DDD/E is the biggest.

You can find both of these measurements with a tape measure or even with a piece of string and a yardstick. (Use the string to get your size, then measure the string against the yardstick.)

To figure out your number size, measure around your chest and ribs with the tape measure or string under your breasts. If you measure an even number, add 4 inches to find your band size. If you measure an odd number, add 5 inches. If you measure 28 inches around, for example, your band size will be 32. If you measure 29 inches, you'll need a size 34 bra.

To find your letter size, measure your chest across your nipples. Now subtract this number from your number size. If the two measurements are the same, you will probably need a AAA or AA cup size. If the difference between the two measurements is 1 inch, your cup size will be A; 2 inches means you're a B; 3 inches means you're a C . . . you've got the idea.

If you're not supershy, ask the salesperson at the lingerie or department store for help in taking these measurements. She should have special measuring equipment and lots of experience. Don't stress—the salesperson can measure your size over your shirt, so you don't have to expose yourself!

Attention, all bra shoppers: Figuring out your bra size is not an exact science. Before you buy, try on the bra and make sure it fits. A bra that fits is comfortable. If you can't take a deep breath or you're popping out of the cup, the bra is too tight. If the cup collapses and looks extrawrinkled, the cup size is too big.

Bras come in lots of different styles. There are special sports bras for sweating on the soccer field. There are bras to make your chest look flatter and bras to make you look bigger. Some bras have wires under the cups (aka underwire bras). Underwire bras can give extra support—especially for larger-sized bosoms. But some women think underwires are really uncomfortable. You can decide for yourself.

If you're stressing about your puny chest, padded or push-up bras may help your breasts look bigger. Stuffing your bra or wearing "falsies" can also help. If you want to experiment, go ahead. But remember, small breasts are nice too. And padded bras only work while you're wearing them.

Your Feelings

Whereas other changes that happen during puberty are more private, your developing breasts are right out there where everyone can see them. If you develop earlier or later than most of your friends, you may feel self-conscious or left out.

No matter where you're at in the breast development department, you may hear about it from immature guys who have nothing better to do. If rude comments or teasing are getting you down, tell a parent or teacher ASAP. Nobody has the right to harass you!

Menstruation: The Basics

Some people call it the curse. Others don't talk about it at all. It's your period (menstruation), and it's really not that big a deal. Our society tends to give it a bad rap, but the truth is that having your period is part of being a girl. It means that someday, when you're ready, you'll be able to get pregnant and have a baby. And that's worth celebrating.

Your First Period

Most girls get their first period between their ninth and sixteenth birthdays. The most common age is thirteen. No one can know in advance when a girl will get her first period. But if you want to play detective, your stage of pubic hair and breast development (see chapter two) can be a good clue. Most girls get their period when they are in stage 3 (about 20 percent) or stage 4 (62 percent). So if you're in stage 1, don't hold your breath, but if you're in stage 4, it could happen any day.

Getting your period means your reproductive

system has kicked into gear. It can take a year or so to get the kinks out, but once your body gets into the rhythm, you'll probably menstruate about once a month. I say *about* once a month because the exact length of the menstrual cycle varies from woman to woman. Most women get their period once every twenty-one to forty days.

Menstruation Information

When you menstruate, a small amount of blood—a few teaspoons a day at most—is released from your uterus through your vagina. Your uterus (aka your womb) is located inside your body between your belly button and your crotch. When a woman gets pregnant, the baby grows in her uterus and comes out through her vagina during birth.

Every month the uterus makes a special lining of tissue that will nourish the embryo (translation: the group of cells that grows into a baby) if the woman gets pregnant. If she doesn't become pregnant, the lining is released, and she gets her period. The next month her uterus will grow a new lining, and the process will start all over again.

Menstruation is closely related to another process known as ovulation. Most girls don't ovulate until they have been menstruating for a while, but in adult women, these two processes work together. Girls are born with two ovaries, which contain hundreds of thousands of tiny ova, or eggs. During ovulation an egg is released from one of the ovaries, and it travels down through the fallopian tube toward the uterus.

All that you need to make a baby is for some sperm (translation: the stuff guys contribute toward making a baby) to meet up with the egg while it's hanging out in the fallopian tube. Usually this happens during sexual intercourse, when a man inserts his penis into a woman's vagina and releases sperm (aka ejaculates). But you can become pregnant if even a teensy-weensy bit of sperm touches the outside of your vagina—sperm are great swimmers. Once you start getting your period (and for some girls, even before), your body is capable of becoming pregnant, so be careful.

Your Feelings

Everyone feels differently about their first period. Some girls are way into it, and others are bummed. Most girls feel a mixture of emotions. Getting your period can be a pain. You'll have to start using tampons or pads, and you may experience cramps or PMS. (See chapter six.) But on the up-side, getting your period means that you are becoming a woman. It doesn't happen all at once, and your body will probably mature long before you're considered a true-blue adult, but getting your period means that you're on your way.

Period Lies ...

 LIE: You shouldn't take a bath or swim during your period.

TRUTH: Swimming and bathing are both OK during your period, but no pads in the pool! Use a tampon when you swim.

 LIE: You should avoid exercise while you're having your period.

TRUTH: Exercise can help fight PMS and ease the pain of menstrual cramps.

 **LIE:** Drinking icy-cold drinks while you're having your period will make you bleed more.

TRUTH: Drinking a lot of liquids, especially water— hot, cold, or in between— is a great way to combat bloating and weight gain during your period.

 LIE: You can't get pregnant during your period.

TRUTH: Having your period does not mean that your body is not fertile. In fact, some girls may be more likely to get pregnant during their period. Don't risk it!

How to Deal with Your Period

If the mere sight of blood makes you swoon, don't freak. Getting your period is not like cutting yourself. Even the wimpiest gals in history have managed to deal with their period. And so will you.

Tampons and Pads

Menstrual blood is not dirty, but it can stain. To protect yourself and your undies, you have two basic choices: tampons and sanitary napkins (aka pads). Both of these products absorb menstrual blood. Tampons absorb the blood while it is still inside of your vagina; pads catch it after it comes out.

Pads

Back when your grandma was a gal, women who used pads had to wear special belts to hold them in place. Today most pads come with adhesive strips, so they stick right to your undies. To use them, you remove the paper from the adhesive strip and press the sticky part of the pad onto your underwear. Wearing a pad may feel weird at first, but most girls get used to it. And don't worry—pads don't show through your clothes, so no one will know you're wearing one.

Pads come in an endless variety of shapes and sizes.

SURPRISE!

We've all heard horror stories about some unfortunate babe who was totally unprepared the first time she got her period. RELAX! Most girls discover their first period while they're going to the bathroom. You might notice a few drops of blood on your undies or a pinkish color on the toilet paper-and that's it!

Don't panic if you're not pre-pared when it happens. Many public bathrooms have vending machines that sell tampons and pads, and every school office has its own stash for surprised students. If all else fails, you can make a "pad" by wadding up some toilet paper andsticking it in your undies.

There are thin pads for days when you're barely bleeding and industrial-strength pads for days when you're gushing. There are pads with flaps that wrap around to protect your undies, and there are others that come individually wrapped so they won't get gross if they wind up at the bottom of your gym bag. Some cost more, and some cost less. Bottom line: They all get the job done.

Menstrual blood starts off clean and odorless, but once it makes contact with germs outside the uterus, it can get smelly. To avoid odor you should change your pad at least every three to four hours—even if you're barely bleeding. To dispose of the used pad, wrap it in some toilet paper and pitch it into the trash. Never, never, never flush pads down the toilet—they'll seriously clog up the plumbing.

Tampons

Tampons are small cylinders of superabsorbent material (usually cotton) that you wear inside your vagina. Some brands come with special applicators for inserting the tampon. With other brands you just use your finger. Fear not—no matter how hard you push the tampon, it can't get lost inside of you. The walls of your vagina and your cervix keep the tampon exactly where you need it. Once the tampon is in place, an attached string hangs out of your vagina. When it's time to take out the tampon, you just tug on the string and—voilà!

Using tampons is a cinch once you get the hang of it. And once they're in, they're so comfy that you'll forget you're wearing one. If the tampon doesn't feel comfortable, you probably haven't inserted it far enough into your vagina.

It is very important to change your tampon at least every three to four hours. And NEVER wear the same one for more than eight hours in a row. It's usually okay to flush used tampons down the toilet unless the plumbing is ancient. Wrappers and plastic applicators go in the trash.

Play It Safe

Women who use tampons increase their risk of developing a rare but serious infection known as toxic shock syndrome (TSS). Most people recover from TSS without any complications. But 8 to 15 percent of women who develop serious cases of TSS die.

The symptoms of TSS include a sudden high fever (over 102°F), aching muscles, vomiting, diarrhea, inflamed eyes, and a rash (kind of like a sunburn). If you have any of these symptoms while using a tampon, take the tampon out and call your doctor or go to the nearest emergency room. Make sure you tell the doctor that you think it could be TSS.

The best way to prevent TSS is to avoid superabsorbent tampons and to change them as often as possible, no matter how little you're bleeding. It's also a good idea to take an occasional tampon break and switch to pads for a few hours a day. Although the ads may tell you otherwise, it's probably best to avoid sleeping with a tampon in (unless you plan to

Read the instructions on the package at least three times before you even think about starting. They put them there for a reason.

Make sure you're aiming for the right place. (It might help to use a handheld mirror.) Once you've got the tampon in your vagina, aim for the small of your back.

It may help to use a brand with an applicator—at least for the first few times.

A bit of K-Y jelly (you'll find it in the drugstore) on the tip of the tampon can help it glide into place more smoothly. (But don't use oil-based products like Vaseline.)

Relax! If you're stressing, your muscles will tighten, and you'll never get it in there. Take your time. You'll get the hang of it!

wake up again in four hours to change it). Also, to keep the area superclean, you should wash your hands both before and after you change your tampon.

PMS **and Cramps**

PMS is shorthand for premenstrual syndrome, and it affects

both body and mind. The physical symptoms of PMS include bloating, weight gain, breast tenderness, pimples, and cravings for sweet or salty foods. The emotional symptoms include depression, nervousness, irritability, and sleep problems. Some women experience either a few or a lot of these symptoms just before they get their period.

No one knows exactly what causes PMS, but there are some things you can do to ease the symptoms.

TIPS FOR DEALING WITH PMS

✔ Cut way down on the sugar and salt. Too much salt can cause weight gain and bloating. Too much sugar can contribute to moodiness and fatigue.

✔ Sweat it out! Regular exercise can help with mood swings, water retention, and cramps. Give it a try, even if you feel like a total slug—you might be surprised at how much better you'll feel afterward.

✔ Over-the-counter pain relievers, especially those with ibuprofen (brand names include Advil and Motrin), can help to ease the pain of cramps. But don't overdo the ibuprofen or aspirin, or you could wind up with an upset stomach.

29

✔ *Avoid or at least cut down on foods and drinks that have caffeine (e.g., coffee, tea, chocolate, and cola)—especially during the two weeks before your period. They can make you more moody and more sensitive to cramps.*

PMS is a big deal to anyone going through it, but fortunately, few women suffer from the full-blown version. Many women get mild symptoms like cramps and moodiness before their period, but these symptoms don't last long, and there are ways to deal. Doctors used to think that PMS affected only older women, but now they know that girls can get it too.

If the tips on page 29 don't help, have a chat with your doc. Many new treatments for PMS exist, and he or she can help you find the best one for you.

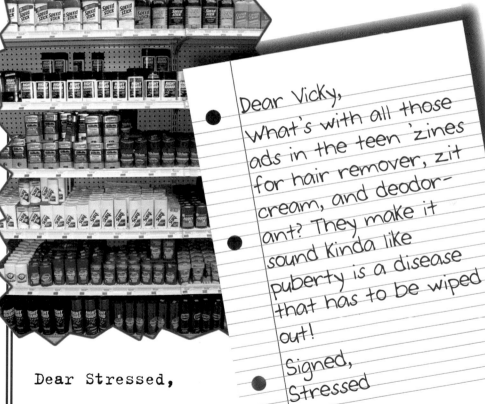

Dear Vicky,

What's with all those ads in the teen 'zines for hair remover, zit cream, and deodorant? They make it sound kinda like puberty is a disease that has to be wiped out!

Signed,
Stressed

Dear Stressed,

If all the hype about pimples and body hair is starting to get to you, you have my permission to chill.

Advertisers (and the magazines and television shows that they sponsor) want you to believe that teenagers are the grossest things on earth—that's how they get you to buy their products. That's not to say that pimples, hairy legs, and body odor are never issues during puberty. They are. But, trust me, you can deal.

Body Odor

As you go through puberty, the sweat glands in your skin will become more active. Certain areas of your body (like your armpits and your palms) have loads of these glands, so you'll sweat even more in these areas. Sweating is not a bad thing. In fact, it's necessary—it's your bod's way of keeping cool. As long as you bathe frequently and wear clean clothes, you'll be fine.

People in many parts of the world stop there. They shower, put on clean clothes, and never think twice about the natural eau de sweat. But most Americans take odor control a step further by using special products to keep themselves smelling extra-rosy. These fall into two categories: Underarm deodorants work by controlling odor, and antiperspirants control how much you sweat in the first place. Some products contain both antiperspirants and deodorants. Be warned that some girls' skin is very sensitive to the chemicals in these products—especially to those with heavy fragrances. Switching to an unscented or hypoallergenic product may help, or try plain baking soda.

News Flash

One place you should never use deodorant is around your vagina. (Ditto for scented tampons and pads.) Vaginal deodorants can seriously irritate the sensitive skin on the vulva. Normally your vagina should smell just fine without any special products. A smelly odor usually means that you have an infection and need to take a trip to the doctor.

Welcome to Zitsville

During puberty the oil glands under the skin's surface become bigger and more active. The white gunk they produce (sebum) is your body's way of keeping your skin moist. But sometimes the oil glands become clogged with extra sebum, and you get blackheads. Clogged ducts are the perfect breeding ground for infection—and then it's welcome to Zitsville.

The truth is that most teens get pimples and acne at

some time during puberty. You can't totally prevent acne, but there are certain things you can do to deal.

✓ Wash your face twice daily with soap and water or a mild cleanser. This helps to remove dirt and dead skin cells that can contribute to acne.

✓ Avoid oil-based cosmetics. They can clog the pores.

✓ Never, ever squeeze your zits. You'll make the infection worse and the zit red and ugly—and you could end up with a nasty scar.

✓ Over-the-counter acne medications can help. (Experiment to see which products work best for you.) But don't go crazy with them, because these products can dry out your skin.

✓ If none of the above works, you should have a chat with your doctor. There are effective treatments for even the most stubborn cases of acne.

FYI: Munching on pizza, chocolate, and french fries probably won't lead to zits. There is no scientific evidence that eating particular foods causes acne. But some girls who are allergic to certain foods (e.g. nuts or chocolate) may break out after eating them. Getting pimples does not mean that you're dirty. Acne has more to do with what is going on inside your skin than what's happening on the surface—where the dirt hangs out.

Although a few pimples never killed anyone (even though you may feel like dying if you run into your crush when you've got a giant zit on your face), more serious acne can be devastating. If left untreated, acne can wreak major havoc not only on your skin (read: mega-scarring) but also on your self-esteem. If this sounds like you, see a doctor ASAP. Most people outgrow even the worst acne, but by the time it clears up, the damage may already be done.

Body Hair

Another sign of puberty is an increase in body hair. You may find more of it on your legs, on your arms, and in your armpits (not to mention pubic hair on your vulva, which we already talked about). Some girls also develop hair on their upper lip, their chin, and the sides of their face.

WARNING: A sudden increase of facial hair may be a sign of a serious illness. Ask around, and if the hairy-lip look does not run in your family or if it came on very suddenly, you should see your doctor. It's probably nothing, but it never hurts to be sure.

For some reason, although both boys and girls develop more body hair during puberty, only the boys are psyched about it. They unbutton their shirts to show off their first strands of chest hair. And they slather on quarts of the smelliest aftershave lotion to make sure that everyone knows they've started shaving. Girls, on the other hand, are often bummed about their newly hairy legs and armpits. Our society tends to view hair on a woman (except, of course, on her head) as unfeminine. But when you think about it, there's no logical reason for this double standard.

Some girls aren't bugged by a little extra fuzz. And hair removal can be a major pain, so it's totally cool if you decide to skip it altogether. Remember, it's your body and your choice. If you decide to go the hair removal route, you have lots of options. Here's the lowdown on hair removal methods:

SHAVING cuts the hair off at the surface of the skin.

Good news: Shaving is easy and doesn't hurt. It tends to be less irritating than other hair removal methods.

Bad news: The hair grows back fast and may appear thicker and darker than it was before you shaved. (It's really not, though.)

Best for: Shaving works well for the legs, underarms, and bikini area. It's too rough for your face. (And I don't advise shaving your pubic hair unless you enjoy feeling really itchy down there.)

Tips: Always use a clean, sharp razor blade and change the blades frequently. Use shaving cream or lotion to avoid razor burn. If you're nervous ask your mom, an older sib, or a more experienced friend for a shaving demo before you try it on your own.

HAIR REMOVAL CREAMS (aka depilatories) contain chemicals that dissolve the hair just below the surface of the skin.

Good news: They're easy and painless to use: You just spread the cream over the hair, wait a few minutes (according to the directions), and then wipe both the cream and the hair away—magic! With depilatories hair takes longer to grow back than with shaving, though not as long as with other methods like waxing.

Bad news: The chemicals can really irritate your skin. And some of them smell yucky.

Best for: Creams can be used almost anywhere on the body. (But avoid underarms.)

Tips: There are various creams made specifically for your face, legs, and bikini area. Make sure you buy the right one for the job. Also, before you try a new product, it's super-important to test it out on a small patch of skin—just the way the package says to do it—to be sure that you don't have a bad reaction.

WAXING works by sticking to the hairs on your skin. When you remove the wax, the hair comes with it.

Good news: The hair takes a while to grow back.

Bad news: OWWWW! It hurts . . . a lot!

owwwww!

Best for: You can use wax almost any-where on your body—but not in your armpits.

Tips: It's best to leave waxing to a professional beautician. If you're a die-hard do-it-yourselfer, though, read the directions carefully (and I mean carefully—as if your life depended on it). There are different kinds of waxes for different body parts—and they don't mix and match.

BLEACHING doesn't remove hair; it just lightens the color so the hair is less noticeable.

Good news: Bleach is less irritating than creams.

Bad news: Bleach is still irritating. If you have dark skin, bleaching is not for you. And some light-skinned gals complain that bleaching turns the hairs orange.

Best for: Bleaching is good for small amounts of hair, like the little fuzzy patches some girls have above their upper lip.

Tips: Read the directions carefully and always use products on the parts of the body that they are made for. (Laundry bleach is *not* an option.) As with creams, do a patch test first.

TWEEZING uses a special tool (tweezers) to pull out individual hairs one at a time.

Good news: It's a cinch to do.

Bad news: It takes a while to nab all those hairs, and it usually hurts a little. Also, the hair grows back pretty quickly.

Best for: Tweezing works best for those stray hairs around the eyebrows. Try to tweeze your legs, and the hair will start growing back before you've finished!

Tips: Tweezing in the direction of the hair growth is faster and less painful.

ELECTROLYSIS uses electric current to kill the hair at the root.

Good news: Once you zap a hair, it will never grow back.

Bad news: Electrolysis is far from painless, and the cost alone is likely to bring tears to your eyes (and your parents').

Best for: This is for people who want permanent hair removal—at any cost.

Tips: Electrolysis should be performed only by a trained technician. Ask your doctor for a recommendation.

EPILATION is similar to electrolysis except that the hair grows back. It is usually done in a salon. If you must do it yourself, have a trained professional teach you how it's done.

EPILIGHT HAIR REMOVAL SYSTEM
WAXING & FACIAL·ELECTROLYSIS

Your Feelings

Whether it's hairy legs or smelly pits, you may feel like your changing body is the grossest thing ever. All of these changes are totally normal and not nearly as yucky as the advertisers would like you to believe. Trust me, as long as you bathe every once in a while, you'll be just fine.

Taking Care of You

If you're feeling a bit overwhelmed, it's OK. You're about to go through some serious changes. But trust me, you'll survive. (Everyone does.) In fact, you might even enjoy yourself.

Puberty is like a roller coaster: On the one hand, it's thrilling and exciting. On the other hand, it can get kinda scary at times. Here are some tips for riding out the rough spots:

Knowledge is power. The more you know about what's in store, the better. Reading books like this one is a great start. (See the By the Book section for other good reads.) But why stop there? Chat with your doctor, your parents, a teacher, or another trusted adult. Ask all of those burning questions. Don't be shy! Remember, they were once your age too.

Don't rush. Everyone has her own puberty timetable. You may be tempted to compare yourself with your pals, but try to remember that puberty is not a race. If you're the last one of your buds to develop, you may feel left out. Trust me, you'll catch up with your pals in no time! If you hit puberty earlier than your friends, you may feel self-conscious or alone. People may assume that because you're physically developed, you're also more mature. But on the inside, you'll probably feel the same as your friends. Remember, it's how you feel (not how you look) that counts.

Get real! Watch television or pick up a teen 'zine, and you'll see skinny models and actresses who look more like little girls than adult women. You'll see people with perfect skin, hair, and makeup. You'll see ads selling products to improve your figure, your face, your hair, and your skin. Don't fall for it! Photographers, advertisers, and TV and movie producers spend a lot of money to make sure that everyone looks totally perfect (and basically the same). In the real world, people look, well, real.

There's no such thing as a perfect body (or face, or hair, or . . . you get the idea). And there's no one way that girls are supposed to look. You may be short or tall, flat-chested or superbusty, shaped like an hourglass or like a Popsicle stick. Everyone is different, and that's what makes real life way more interesting than a magazine. And it's true that some people make judgments about you based on the way you look—but that's their problem. Don't make it yours.

Be yourself. Part of growing up is getting to know yourself and finding your special place in the world. You may also find that your pals are more important than they ever were before. It's natural to want to compare yourself with them. And you may start to get nervous if you feel different from the group. But remember, everyone is different. That's what makes the world an interesting place to be. You're an individual, and that's what makes you special.

areolas The rings of skin, usually reddish or dark in color, around the nipples.

embryo A group of cells from which a baby will develop.

fallopian tubes Two tubes inside the female body that connect the ovaries to the uterus.

media Newspapers, magazines, television, radio, and other types of communication that reach large numbers of people.

menstruation The monthly shedding of the lining of a woman's uterus, which occurs each month unless a woman becomes pregnant.

ovaries A pair of organs in the female body that produce ova, or eggs.

premenstrual syndrome (PMS) A group of emotional and physical changes that some girls and women experience before their monthly period.

puberty A stage during which boys' and girls' bodies begin to take on adult characteristics and become physically able to reproduce, or produce babies.

pubic hair Hair that first appears during puberty on the sex organs and the pubic region (the area below the belly button and above the sex organs).

sebum An oily material produced by glands in the skin. During puberty the body may produce extra sebum, which can lead to acne.

sperm The male cells that unite with a female's eggs to produce a baby.

toxic shock syndrome (TSS) A disease that can be caused by the use of tampons during menstruation.

uterus An organ in the female body in which babies develop before birth.

vulva The outer part of the vagina.

It's a Girl's World:
helpful info

Web Sites
Girlspace
http://www.kotex.com/girlspace

gURL (on-line 'zine)
http://www.gURL.com

KidsHealth.org
www.kidshealth.org/kid/

PMS Palace—The Monthly Ranting Place (on-line message board
www.insidetheweb.com/mbs.cgi/mb181066

Puberty Page
http://members.xoom.com/puberty

The Puberty Palace—Just for Girls (on-line message board)
http://www.insidetheweb.com/mbs.cgi/mb320789

Virtual Kid's Puberty 101
www.virtualkid.com/p101_menu.html

Magazines
New Moon: The Magazine for Girls and Their Dreams
This awesome magazine is written and produced by a group of
girls ages eight to fourteen.

By the Book:
further reading

Blume, Judy. *Are You There God? It's Me, Margaret.* New York: Bantam Doubleday Dell Books for Young Readers, 1971.

Bourgeois, Paulette, and Martin Wolfish. *Changes in You & Me: A Book About Puberty, Mostly for Girls.* Kansas City, MO: Andrews & McMeel, 1994.

Golliher, Catherine. *Puberty and Reproduction.* Santa Cruz, CA: ETR Associates, 1996.

Harlan, Judith. *Girl Talk: Staying Strong, Feeling Good, Sticking Together.* New York: Walker Publishing Co., 1997.

Jukes, Mavis. *It's a Girl Thing.* New York: Alfred A. Knopf, 1996.

Madaras, Lynda, and Area Madaras. *My Body, Myself for Girls.* New York: Newmarket Press, 1993.

————. *What's Happening to My Body Book for Girls.* New York: Newmarket Press, 1998.

Roehm, Michelle, ed. *Girls Know Best: Advice for Girls from Girls on Just About Everything.* Hillsboro, OR: Beyond Words Publishing, 1997.

Schaefer, Valorie Lee. *The Care and Keeping of You: The Body Book for Girls.* Middleton, WI: Pleasant Company Publications, 1998.

Index

Credits

About the Author

Victoria Shaw received her Ph.D. in psychology from Princeton University. She has taught classes in child development at Teachers College of Columbia University and conducted research concerning adolescents. She has also participated in Big Brothers/Big Sisters and served as a social work intern in Connecticut. Ms. Shaw and her family live in New York City.

Photo Credits

Cover photo by Scott Bauer; pp. 6, 11, 16 © 1999 Bryson Biomedical Illustration/Custom Medical Stock Photo; pp. 7, 13, 23, 28, 35, 37, 43 by Debra L. Rothenberg; pp. 10, 11 © LifeART Super Anatomy Copyright © 1994 TechPool Studios Corp. USA; pp. 14, 20 by John Bentham; pp. 15, 17, 18, 19, 32, 34, 37, 38, 39 by Scott Bauer; pp. 17, 19, 24, 25, 26, 31, 34, 40 by Cappie Hotchkiss; pp. 21, 22 © 1999 June Hill Pedigo/Custom Medical Stock Photo; p. 42 by Les Mills

Design and Layout

Laura Murawski